50 Tokyo at Home Recipes

By: Kelly Johnson

Table of Contents

- Homemade Miso Soup
- Teriyaki Chicken Rice Bowl
- Sushi Rolls (Maki and Nigiri)
- Tempura Shrimp and Vegetables
- Okonomiyaki (Japanese Pancake)
- Tonkatsu (Breaded Pork Cutlet)
- Japanese Beef Curry
- Gyoza (Dumplings)
- Ramen with Shoyu Broth
- Ebi Fry (Fried Shrimp)
- Katsudon (Pork Cutlet Rice Bowl)
- Tofu Katsu
- Udon Noodles in Broth
- Japanese Cheesecake
- Onigiri (Rice Balls)
- Teriyaki Salmon
- Yaki Udon (Stir-Fried Noodles)

- Bento Box with Chicken Karaage
- Shabu Shabu (Japanese Hot Pot)
- Chawanmushi (Savory Egg Custard)
- Zaru Soba (Cold Buckwheat Noodles)
- Donburi (Rice Bowl with Toppings)
- Tamagoyaki (Japanese Omelette)
- Maki Sushi (Rolled Sushi)
- Oyakodon (Chicken and Egg Rice Bowl)
- Takoyaki (Octopus Balls)
- Gyu Don (Beef Rice Bowl)
- Katsu Curry (Curry with Pork Cutlet)
- Soba Salad with Sesame Dressing
- Miso-Glazed Eggplant
- Oden (Hot Pot)
- Yaki Imo (Roasted Sweet Potato)
- Karaage (Japanese Fried Chicken)
- Japanese-style Grilled Fish
- Kaki Fry (Fried Oysters)
- Ramen with Tonkotsu Broth

- Japanese Potato Salad
- Katsu Sando (Pork Cutlet Sandwich)
- Hiyayakko (Chilled Tofu)
- Mochi with Red Bean Paste
- Tempura Udon
- Japanese-Style Beef Stew
- Hokkaido-style Corn Soup
- Okonomiyaki with Shrimp and Veggies
- Niku Miso (Beef and Miso Stir-fry)
- Spicy Tuna Poke Bowl
- Oyakodon with Teriyaki Sauce
- Chashu Pork for Ramen
- Kushi Katsu (Skewered Fried Meats)
- Matcha Latte and Mochi Desserts

Homemade Miso Soup

Ingredients:

- 4 cups dashi (or substitute with vegetable broth)
- 3 tbsp miso paste (white or red)
- 1/2 block tofu, cubed
- 1/4 cup green onions, chopped
- 1/4 cup wakame seaweed (optional)

Instructions:

1. In a pot, bring dashi (or broth) to a simmer over medium heat.
2. Whisk in the miso paste until dissolved.
3. Add tofu and wakame seaweed (if using) and cook for another 2-3 minutes.
4. Garnish with chopped green onions and serve hot!

Teriyaki Chicken Rice Bowl

Ingredients:

- 2 chicken breasts or thighs
- 1/4 cup soy sauce
- 2 tbsp honey or brown sugar
- 1 tbsp rice vinegar
- 1 tbsp sesame oil
- 1 clove garlic, minced
- Cooked white rice
- Steamed vegetables (broccoli, carrots, etc.)

Instructions:

1. In a bowl, whisk together soy sauce, honey, rice vinegar, sesame oil, and garlic.
2. Marinate the chicken in the sauce for 15-20 minutes.
3. Grill or pan-fry the chicken until fully cooked (about 6-7 minutes per side).
4. Serve the chicken over rice and top with steamed vegetables. Drizzle with additional teriyaki sauce.

Sushi Rolls (Maki and Nigiri)

Ingredients:

- 1 cup sushi rice
- 2 cups water
- 2 tbsp rice vinegar
- 1 tbsp sugar
- 1/2 tsp salt
- Nori sheets
- Fish of choice (tuna, salmon, etc.) or veggies (cucumber, avocado, etc.)
- Soy sauce for dipping

Instructions:

1. Rinse sushi rice until water runs clear, then cook according to package instructions.
2. Mix rice vinegar, sugar, and salt in a bowl, then stir into the cooked rice. Let it cool.
3. For maki rolls, place nori on a bamboo mat, spread a thin layer of rice, and add fillings (fish, avocado, cucumber). Roll tightly and slice into pieces.
4. For nigiri, form small rice balls and top with thin slices of fish.
5. Serve with soy sauce, wasabi, and pickled ginger.

Tempura Shrimp and Vegetables

Ingredients:

- 10 large shrimp, peeled and deveined
- 1 zucchini, sliced
- 1 sweet potato, thinly sliced
- 1 cup tempura batter mix (or make your own with flour and cold water)
- Oil for frying
- Salt for seasoning

Instructions:

1. Prepare the tempura batter according to package instructions.
2. Heat oil in a deep fryer or large pot to 350°F (175°C).
3. Dip shrimp and vegetables into the batter, then fry in batches until golden and crispy, about 2-3 minutes.
4. Drain on paper towels and season with salt. Serve with dipping sauce.

Okonomiyaki (Japanese Pancake)

Ingredients:

- 1 cup all-purpose flour
- 1/2 cup dashi (or water)
- 1 egg
- 1/2 cup shredded cabbage
- 1/4 cup green onions, chopped
- 1/4 cup cooked shrimp or pork (optional)
- Okonomiyaki sauce (or Worcestershire sauce)
- Kewpie mayonnaise

Instructions:

1. In a bowl, mix flour, dashi, and egg until smooth.
2. Add cabbage, green onions, and optional protein (shrimp or pork).
3. Heat a pan over medium heat and pour the batter to form a pancake. Cook for 3-4 minutes on each side until golden and crispy.
4. Drizzle with okonomiyaki sauce and a swirl of mayonnaise before serving.

Tonkatsu (Breaded Pork Cutlet)

Ingredients:

- 2 pork chops (boneless)
- 1 cup panko breadcrumbs
- 1/2 cup flour
- 1 egg, beaten
- Salt and pepper to taste
- Oil for frying
- Tonkatsu sauce for serving

Instructions:

1. Season the pork chops with salt and pepper.
2. Dredge the pork in flour, dip in egg, then coat in panko breadcrumbs.
3. Heat oil in a pan over medium heat and fry the pork for 4-5 minutes on each side until crispy and golden.
4. Serve with tonkatsu sauce and rice.

Japanese Beef Curry

Ingredients:

- 1 lb beef stew meat
- 1 onion, chopped
- 2 carrots, sliced
- 2 potatoes, peeled and cubed
- 1/2 cup curry roux (store-bought or homemade)
- 4 cups beef broth
- Salt and pepper to taste

Instructions:

1. Brown the beef in a pot over medium heat. Remove and set aside.
2. Add onions to the pot and sauté until softened.
3. Add carrots, potatoes, and beef broth. Bring to a boil and simmer for 20-25 minutes.
4. Stir in the curry roux and continue to simmer until thickened. Season with salt and pepper.
5. Serve over steamed rice.

Gyoza (Dumplings)

Ingredients:

- 1/2 lb ground pork or chicken
- 1/4 cup cabbage, finely chopped
- 1/4 cup green onions, chopped
- 1 clove garlic, minced
- 1 tbsp soy sauce
- 1 tsp sesame oil
- 1 pack gyoza wrappers

Instructions:

1. Mix the ground meat, cabbage, green onions, garlic, soy sauce, and sesame oil in a bowl.
2. Place a small spoonful of filling onto each gyoza wrapper. Moisten the edges and fold into a half-moon shape.
3. Heat a skillet over medium heat and add a little oil. Place the gyoza in the skillet and cook until the bottoms are golden.
4. Add a small amount of water and cover to steam for 3-4 minutes. Serve with soy sauce for dipping.

Ramen with Shoyu Broth

Ingredients:

- 4 cups chicken or vegetable broth
- 1/4 cup soy sauce
- 1 tbsp mirin
- 2 tbsp miso paste
- 2 ramen noodle packets
- 2 soft-boiled eggs
- Toppings: sliced pork, green onions, bamboo shoots, nori, etc.

Instructions:

1. In a pot, combine broth, soy sauce, mirin, and miso paste. Bring to a simmer for 10 minutes.
2. Cook the ramen noodles according to the package instructions and set aside.
3. Divide the noodles between bowls, pour the broth over the noodles, and top with your choice of toppings.
4. Serve hot!

Ebi Fry (Fried Shrimp)

Ingredients:

- 12 large shrimp, peeled and deveined
- 1 cup panko breadcrumbs
- 1/2 cup flour
- 1 egg, beaten
- Oil for frying
- Lemon wedges and tartar sauce for serving

Instructions:

1. Dredge the shrimp in flour, dip in egg, and coat with panko breadcrumbs.
2. Heat oil in a pan to 350°F (175°C) and fry the shrimp until golden, about 3-4 minutes.
3. Drain on paper towels and serve with lemon wedges and tartar sauce.

Katsudon (Pork Cutlet Rice Bowl)

Ingredients:

- 2 tonkatsu pork cutlets (prepared earlier)
- 1/2 cup onion, sliced
- 1/4 cup soy sauce
- 1/4 cup mirin
- 1 egg, beaten
- 2 cups steamed rice

Instructions:

1. Heat soy sauce and mirin in a skillet. Add onions and cook until softened.
2. Place the tonkatsu cutlets in the pan, pour the egg over, and cook until the egg is set.
3. Serve the pork and egg mixture over steamed rice.

Tofu Katsu

Ingredients:

- 1 block firm tofu, pressed and sliced
- 1 cup panko breadcrumbs
- 1/2 cup flour
- 1 egg (or egg replacer for vegan version)
- Salt and pepper to taste
- Oil for frying
- Tonkatsu sauce for serving

Instructions:

1. Season the tofu slices with salt and pepper.
2. Dredge tofu in flour, dip into the beaten egg, then coat in panko breadcrumbs.
3. Heat oil in a pan over medium heat and fry tofu until golden brown on both sides, about 4-5 minutes.
4. Serve with tonkatsu sauce.

Udon Noodles in Broth

Ingredients:

- 4 cups dashi (or vegetable broth)
- 1 tbsp soy sauce
- 1 tbsp mirin
- 1 tsp sugar
- 2 servings udon noodles
- Toppings: green onions, soft-boiled egg, tempura, kamaboko (fish cake)

Instructions:

1. In a pot, bring dashi, soy sauce, mirin, and sugar to a simmer.
2. Cook udon noodles according to package instructions and drain.
3. Divide the noodles into bowls and pour the broth over them.
4. Top with your choice of toppings, such as green onions, a soft-boiled egg, or tempura.

Japanese Cheesecake

Ingredients:

- 8 oz cream cheese, softened
- 1/2 cup sugar
- 1/4 cup milk
- 4 eggs, separated
- 1/4 cup all-purpose flour
- 1/4 cup cornstarch
- 1 tsp vanilla extract
- 1/4 tsp cream of tartar

Instructions:

1. Preheat your oven to 320°F (160°C) and grease a cake pan.
2. Beat the cream cheese and sugar together until smooth. Add milk, egg yolks, flour, cornstarch, and vanilla. Mix well.
3. In a separate bowl, beat egg whites with cream of tartar until stiff peaks form.
4. Gently fold the egg whites into the cream cheese mixture.
5. Pour the batter into the prepared pan and bake for 45-50 minutes or until set. Let cool before serving.

Onigiri (Rice Balls)

Ingredients:

- 2 cups cooked sushi rice
- 1 tbsp rice vinegar
- 1 tsp sugar
- 1/2 tsp salt
- Fillings: umeboshi (pickled plum), tuna mayo, or cooked salmon
- Nori (seaweed) for wrapping

Instructions:

1. Mix the rice vinegar, sugar, and salt into the cooked rice while it's still warm.
2. Wet your hands and take a small portion of rice. Flatten it slightly and place a teaspoon of filling in the center.
3. Shape the rice into a triangle or ball and wrap with a strip of nori.
4. Serve as a snack or with meals.

Teriyaki Salmon

Ingredients:

- 2 salmon fillets
- 1/4 cup soy sauce
- 2 tbsp mirin
- 2 tbsp honey
- 1 tbsp rice vinegar
- 1 tsp grated ginger
- 1 garlic clove, minced

Instructions:

1. In a bowl, whisk together soy sauce, mirin, honey, rice vinegar, ginger, and garlic.
2. Marinate the salmon fillets in the teriyaki sauce for 15-20 minutes.
3. Heat a pan over medium heat and cook the salmon for 4-5 minutes per side until cooked through.
4. Serve with rice and steamed vegetables, drizzling with leftover teriyaki sauce.

Yaki Udon (Stir-Fried Noodles)

Ingredients:

- 2 servings udon noodles
- 1 tbsp soy sauce
- 1 tbsp oyster sauce
- 1 tsp sesame oil
- 1/2 onion, sliced
- 1 carrot, julienned
- 1/2 bell pepper, sliced
- 2-3 mushrooms, sliced
- Green onions for garnish

Instructions:

1. Cook udon noodles according to the package instructions and set aside.
2. In a large pan, heat sesame oil and sauté the onion, carrot, bell pepper, and mushrooms until tender.
3. Add the noodles to the pan and stir-fry with soy sauce, oyster sauce, and a little more sesame oil until heated through.
4. Garnish with green onions and serve.

Bento Box with Chicken Karaage

Ingredients:

- 2 chicken thighs, boneless and skinless, cut into bite-sized pieces
- 1/4 cup soy sauce
- 1 tbsp mirin
- 1 tbsp sake
- 1 tsp grated ginger
- 1/2 cup flour
- 1/4 cup cornstarch
- Oil for frying
- Cooked rice, pickled vegetables, and fruit for serving

Instructions:

1. Mix soy sauce, mirin, sake, and ginger to marinate the chicken for 30 minutes.
2. Combine flour and cornstarch in a bowl. Dredge marinated chicken in the flour mixture.
3. Heat oil in a pan and fry the chicken until crispy and golden, about 4-5 minutes per side.
4. Assemble the bento box with chicken karaage, rice, pickled vegetables, and fruit.

Shabu Shabu (Japanese Hot Pot)

Ingredients:

- 1 lb thinly sliced beef (ribeye or sirloin)
- 6 cups dashi (or vegetable broth)
- 1 tbsp soy sauce
- 1 tbsp mirin
- 1/2 cup sliced mushrooms
- 1/2 cup napa cabbage, chopped
- 1/2 cup tofu, cubed
- 1 cup udon noodles or cooked rice

Instructions:

1. In a hot pot, bring dashi, soy sauce, and mirin to a simmer.
2. Add mushrooms, cabbage, and tofu to the broth.
3. Cook the thinly sliced beef in the hot broth for a few seconds until just done.
4. Dip the beef into the broth and serve with dipping sauces (ponzu, sesame sauce) and noodles or rice.

Chawanmushi (Savory Egg Custard)

Ingredients:

- 4 eggs
- 2 cups dashi (or chicken broth)
- 1 tbsp soy sauce
- 1 tbsp mirin
- 1/2 tsp salt
- Shrimp, mushrooms, or ginkgo nuts for filling

Instructions:

1. Beat eggs in a bowl and add dashi, soy sauce, mirin, and salt.
2. Strain the mixture to remove any air bubbles.
3. Pour into small cups and add a few shrimp or vegetables.
4. Steam the custard over medium heat for 15-20 minutes until set.

Zaru Soba (Cold Buckwheat Noodles)

Ingredients:

- 2 servings soba noodles
- 1/4 cup soy sauce
- 1/4 cup mirin
- 1/4 cup water
- 1 tsp sugar
- Wasabi and sliced green onions for garnish

Instructions:

1. Cook soba noodles according to package instructions and rinse under cold water.
2. In a small bowl, combine soy sauce, mirin, water, and sugar to make the dipping sauce.
3. Serve the cold noodles with dipping sauce, wasabi, and sliced green onions on the side.

Donburi (Rice Bowl with Toppings)

Ingredients:

- 2 cups cooked rice
- Toppings: teriyaki chicken, beef, fried egg, pickled vegetables, or vegetables of choice
- Soy sauce or teriyaki sauce for drizzling

Instructions:

1. Place the rice in bowls.
2. Add your choice of toppings (teriyaki chicken, beef, or a fried egg).
3. Drizzle with soy sauce or teriyaki sauce and serve immediately.

Tamagoyaki (Japanese Omelette)

Ingredients:

- 4 eggs
- 1 tbsp soy sauce
- 1 tsp mirin
- 1 tsp sugar
- 1 tbsp oil for frying

Instructions:

1. In a bowl, whisk the eggs with soy sauce, mirin, and sugar.
2. Heat a small, rectangular or square frying pan over medium-low heat and lightly oil it.
3. Pour a thin layer of the egg mixture into the pan, swirling to coat.
4. Once the egg is set but still slightly runny, roll it up into a log and push it to one side of the pan.
5. Add another thin layer of egg, rolling the previous log into the new layer.
6. Repeat the process until all the eggs are used, then remove and slice into pieces.

Maki Sushi (Rolled Sushi)

Ingredients:

- 2 cups sushi rice, cooked and seasoned
- 4-5 nori (seaweed) sheets
- Fillings: cucumber, avocado, tuna, or salmon
- Soy sauce, wasabi, and pickled ginger for serving

Instructions:

1. Lay a nori sheet on a bamboo sushi mat.
2. Wet your hands and spread a thin layer of sushi rice over the nori, leaving a 1-inch border at the top.
3. Add your choice of fillings (cucumber, avocado, fish).
4. Roll the sushi tightly using the bamboo mat, sealing the edge with a little water.
5. Slice into pieces and serve with soy sauce, wasabi, and pickled ginger.

Oyakodon (Chicken and Egg Rice Bowl)

Ingredients:

- 2 chicken thighs, thinly sliced
- 1 onion, sliced
- 2 eggs, beaten
- 2 cups cooked rice
- 1/4 cup soy sauce
- 1/4 cup mirin
- 1 tbsp sugar
- 1/4 cup dashi (or water)

Instructions:

1. In a pan, cook the chicken and onions with a little oil until the chicken is browned.
2. Add the soy sauce, mirin, sugar, and dashi to the pan. Simmer for 10 minutes.
3. Pour in the beaten eggs and cook until just set.
4. Serve over a bowl of cooked rice.

Takoyaki (Octopus Balls)

Ingredients:

- 1/2 lb cooked octopus, diced
- 1 cup takoyaki flour (or substitute with pancake mix)
- 1 egg
- 1/2 cup dashi or water
- 1/4 cup green onions, chopped
- Pickled ginger, chopped
- Oil for frying
- Takoyaki sauce and bonito flakes for topping

Instructions:

1. Mix takoyaki flour, egg, and dashi or water into a batter.
2. Heat a takoyaki pan and grease each hole with oil.
3. Pour the batter into the holes, add a piece of octopus, a little green onion, and pickled ginger.
4. Once the batter sets, flip the balls to cook on all sides.
5. Serve with takoyaki sauce and bonito flakes.

Gyu Don (Beef Rice Bowl)

Ingredients:

- 1/2 lb beef (flank steak or sirloin), thinly sliced
- 1 onion, sliced
- 1/4 cup soy sauce
- 1/4 cup mirin
- 1 tbsp sugar
- 2 cups cooked rice
- 1/4 cup dashi or water

Instructions:

1. In a pan, sauté the onions until softened.
2. Add the beef, soy sauce, mirin, sugar, and dashi. Simmer for 10 minutes.
3. Serve over a bowl of hot rice.

Katsu Curry (Curry with Pork Cutlet)

Ingredients:

- 2 pork cutlets (for tonkatsu)
- 1 cup panko breadcrumbs
- 1 egg, beaten
- 1/2 cup flour
- 1 pack Japanese curry roux
- 2 potatoes, peeled and diced
- 1 carrot, sliced
- 2 cups water
- Cooked rice

Instructions:

1. Bread the pork cutlets by dipping them in flour, egg, and panko breadcrumbs. Fry in oil until golden and cooked through.
2. In a separate pot, cook the potatoes and carrots in water until tender.
3. Add the curry roux and simmer until the sauce thickens.
4. Serve the pork cutlets over rice, topped with curry sauce.

Soba Salad with Sesame Dressing

Ingredients:

- 2 cups soba noodles, cooked and cooled
- 1 cucumber, julienned
- 1 carrot, julienned
- 2 tbsp sesame oil
- 1 tbsp soy sauce
- 1 tbsp rice vinegar
- 1 tsp sugar
- 1 tbsp sesame seeds

Instructions:

1. Mix sesame oil, soy sauce, rice vinegar, and sugar to make the dressing.
2. Toss the cooked soba noodles, cucumber, and carrot with the dressing.
3. Garnish with sesame seeds before serving.

Miso-Glazed Eggplant

Ingredients:

- 2 eggplants, sliced
- 3 tbsp miso paste
- 1 tbsp soy sauce
- 1 tbsp mirin
- 1 tsp sugar
- 1 tbsp sesame oil

Instructions:

1. Mix miso paste, soy sauce, mirin, sugar, and sesame oil into a glaze.
2. Brush the eggplant slices with the glaze and roast them at 375°F (190°C) for 20-25 minutes until tender and caramelized.
3. Serve with steamed rice.

Oden (Hot Pot)

Ingredients:

- 4 cups dashi or vegetable broth
- 2 boiled eggs
- 2 pieces konjac (konnyaku)
- 2 pieces daikon radish, sliced
- 1/2 lb tofu, cut into squares
- 2-3 fish cakes (kamaboko)
- 1 tbsp soy sauce
- 1 tbsp mirin

Instructions:

1. Heat the dashi in a pot and add soy sauce and mirin.
2. Add all the ingredients into the pot and simmer for 30-40 minutes.
3. Serve hot with mustard on the side.

Yaki Imo (Roasted Sweet Potato)

Ingredients:

- 2 Japanese sweet potatoes (satsumaimo)

Instructions:

1. Preheat your oven to 400°F (200°C).
2. Wash the sweet potatoes and poke a few holes in them with a fork.
3. Roast for 45-60 minutes until soft and tender.
4. Serve hot or cold.

Karaage (Japanese Fried Chicken)

Ingredients:

- 2 chicken thighs, boneless and skinless, cut into bite-sized pieces
- 2 tbsp soy sauce
- 1 tbsp sake
- 1 tsp ginger, grated
- 1 clove garlic, minced
- 1/2 cup potato starch or cornstarch
- Oil for frying

Instructions:

1. Marinate the chicken pieces with soy sauce, sake, ginger, and garlic for 30 minutes.
2. Coat the chicken with potato starch.
3. Fry in oil until crispy and golden, about 5-6 minutes per side.
4. Serve with a side of lemon wedges and dipping sauce.

Japanese-style Grilled Fish

Ingredients:

- 2 whole fish (like mackerel or saba), cleaned and gutted
- 2 tbsp soy sauce
- 1 tbsp mirin
- 1 tbsp sake
- 1 tsp sugar
- 1/2 tsp sesame oil

Instructions:

1. Mix soy sauce, mirin, sake, sugar, and sesame oil to make a marinade.
2. Brush the fish with the marinade and let it sit for 20-30 minutes.
3. Grill the fish on medium heat until golden brown and cooked through, about 5-7 minutes on each side.
4. Serve with steamed rice and a side of pickled vegetables.

Kaki Fry (Fried Oysters)

Ingredients:

- 12 fresh oysters, shucked
- 1/2 cup flour
- 1 egg, beaten
- 1/2 cup panko breadcrumbs
- Salt and pepper to taste
- Oil for frying

Instructions:

1. Season the oysters with salt and pepper.
2. Dredge them in flour, dip in the beaten egg, and coat with panko breadcrumbs.
3. Heat oil in a pan over medium-high heat. Fry the oysters until golden and crispy, about 3-4 minutes.
4. Serve with tonkatsu sauce and a wedge of lemon.

Ramen with Tonkotsu Broth

Ingredients:

- 4 cups pork bones or pork stock
- 2 tbsp soy sauce
- 1 tbsp miso paste
- 2 garlic cloves, minced
- 1-inch piece of ginger, sliced
- 2 spring onions, chopped
- Ramen noodles
- Toppings: boiled egg, chashu pork, nori, bamboo shoots, and sesame seeds

Instructions:

1. Simmer the pork bones with water, garlic, and ginger for 4-5 hours to create a rich, creamy tonkotsu broth.
2. Strain the broth and stir in soy sauce and miso paste.
3. Cook the ramen noodles according to package instructions.
4. Serve the noodles in a bowl with the tonkotsu broth and your choice of toppings.

Japanese Potato Salad

Ingredients:

- 3 medium potatoes, boiled and mashed
- 1/4 cup mayonnaise
- 1/4 cup rice vinegar
- 1/2 cucumber, julienned
- 1/4 cup grated carrot
- Salt and pepper to taste

Instructions:

1. Boil the potatoes until tender, then mash them with a fork.
2. In a bowl, combine the mashed potatoes with mayonnaise, rice vinegar, cucumber, and grated carrot.
3. Season with salt and pepper, and chill in the fridge for at least 30 minutes before serving.

Katsu Sando (Pork Cutlet Sandwich)

Ingredients:

- 2 slices of white bread
- 1 pork cutlet (breaded and fried)
- 1 tbsp tonkatsu sauce
- Cabbage (shredded)
- 1 tbsp mayonnaise

Instructions:

1. Fry the pork cutlet until golden brown and crispy.
2. Toast the bread lightly and spread mayonnaise on one side of each slice.
3. Place the pork cutlet on one slice, drizzle with tonkatsu sauce, and top with shredded cabbage.
4. Close the sandwich and cut in half. Serve immediately.

Hiyayakko (Chilled Tofu)

Ingredients:

- 1 block of silken tofu
- 1 tbsp soy sauce
- 1 tsp sesame oil
- 1 tbsp chopped spring onions
- A sprinkle of bonito flakes (optional)
- A dash of grated ginger

Instructions:

1. Cut the tofu into cubes and place in a small bowl.
2. Drizzle with soy sauce and sesame oil.
3. Top with chopped spring onions, bonito flakes, and grated ginger.
4. Serve chilled as a refreshing side dish or appetizer.

Mochi with Red Bean Paste

Ingredients:

- 1 cup mochiko (sweet rice flour)
- 1/2 cup water
- 1/4 cup sugar
- 1/2 cup red bean paste (anko)

Instructions:

1. Mix mochiko, water, and sugar in a bowl until smooth.
2. Steam the mixture for 15-20 minutes until it becomes a sticky dough.
3. Let it cool slightly, then divide the dough into small portions.
4. Flatten each portion and place a small amount of red bean paste in the center, then wrap the dough around the paste and roll into a ball.
5. Dust with cornstarch or potato starch to prevent sticking and serve.

Tempura Udon

Ingredients:

- 2 servings udon noodles
- 1 cup dashi (or water)
- 2 tbsp soy sauce
- 1 tbsp mirin
- 6 pieces of tempura (shrimp, sweet potato, or vegetables)
- Spring onions and sesame seeds for garnish

Instructions:

1. Cook the udon noodles according to package instructions.
2. In a separate pot, combine dashi, soy sauce, and mirin, and bring to a simmer.
3. Place the cooked noodles in a bowl and pour the broth over them.
4. Top with tempura, spring onions, and sesame seeds. Serve immediately.

Japanese-Style Beef Stew

Ingredients:

- 1 lb beef stew meat, cubed
- 2 carrots, chopped
- 1 onion, chopped
- 2 potatoes, peeled and cubed
- 3 cups beef broth
- 1 tbsp soy sauce
- 1 tbsp mirin
- 1 tbsp sake
- 1 tbsp sugar
- Salt and pepper to taste

Instructions:

1. Brown the beef cubes in a pot over medium heat.
2. Add the onions and cook until softened.
3. Pour in the beef broth, soy sauce, mirin, sake, sugar, and season with salt and pepper.
4. Bring to a boil, then reduce heat and simmer for 1.5-2 hours until the beef is tender.
5. Add the carrots and potatoes and cook for an additional 30 minutes until everything is tender.

6. Serve hot with steamed rice.

Hokkaido-style Corn Soup

Ingredients:

- 2 cups sweet corn (frozen or fresh)
- 2 cups milk
- 1/2 cup heavy cream
- 1 tbsp butter
- Salt and pepper to taste
- 1 tbsp chopped spring onions for garnish

Instructions:

1. In a pot, melt the butter and add the corn. Cook for a few minutes.
2. Add the milk and heavy cream, and bring to a simmer. Let it cook for 10-15 minutes, stirring occasionally.
3. Blend the soup until smooth, then season with salt and pepper.
4. Serve hot, garnished with chopped spring onions.

Okonomiyaki with Shrimp and Veggies

Ingredients:

- 1 cup all-purpose flour
- 1/2 cup dashi (or water)
- 1 egg
- 1 cup cabbage, shredded
- 1/2 cup shrimp, peeled and chopped
- 1/4 cup green onions, chopped
- 1/4 cup carrots, julienned
- 2 tbsp soy sauce
- 1 tbsp sesame oil
- Okonomiyaki sauce (or tonkatsu sauce)
- Japanese mayonnaise (Kewpie)

Instructions:

1. In a bowl, mix flour, dashi, and egg until smooth.
2. Add the cabbage, shrimp, green onions, and carrots to the batter. Mix well.
3. Heat sesame oil in a pan over medium heat and pour the batter into the pan to form a pancake.
4. Cook for 4-5 minutes on each side until golden brown and cooked through.
5. Top with Okonomiyaki sauce and drizzle with Japanese mayonnaise. Serve hot!

Niku Miso (Beef and Miso Stir-fry)

Ingredients:

- 1 lb thinly sliced beef (like ribeye or sirloin)
- 1 onion, thinly sliced
- 2 tbsp miso paste
- 2 tbsp soy sauce
- 1 tbsp mirin
- 1 tbsp sake
- 1 tbsp sugar
- 1 tbsp vegetable oil
- 1/2 cup water
- 1/2 tsp ground pepper
- Green onions for garnish

Instructions:

1. Heat oil in a pan and stir-fry the sliced beef until browned.
2. Add onions and continue to cook until softened.
3. In a small bowl, mix miso paste, soy sauce, mirin, sake, sugar, and water to make the sauce.
4. Pour the sauce over the beef and onions, and simmer for 5-7 minutes until everything is well coated and the sauce thickens.

5. Garnish with green onions and serve with steamed rice.

Spicy Tuna Poke Bowl

Ingredients:

- 1 lb sushi-grade tuna, diced
- 2 tbsp soy sauce
- 1 tbsp sesame oil
- 1 tbsp rice vinegar
- 1 tsp sriracha (or more for heat)
- 1/2 avocado, sliced
- 1/4 cup cucumber, sliced
- 1/4 cup radishes, sliced
- 1/4 cup edamame (optional)
- Cooked rice (for serving)
- Seaweed flakes for garnish
- Sesame seeds for garnish

Instructions:

1. In a bowl, combine tuna with soy sauce, sesame oil, rice vinegar, and sriracha. Toss to coat and marinate for 10 minutes.
2. Serve the marinated tuna on top of cooked rice.
3. Top with avocado, cucumber, radishes, and edamame.
4. Garnish with seaweed flakes and sesame seeds before serving.

Oyakodon with Teriyaki Sauce

Ingredients:

- 2 chicken breasts or thighs, cut into bite-sized pieces
- 2 eggs, beaten
- 1 onion, sliced
- 1 tbsp soy sauce
- 1 tbsp mirin
- 1 tbsp sugar
- 1 tbsp sake
- 1 tbsp teriyaki sauce
- Steamed rice (for serving)
- Green onions for garnish

Instructions:

1. In a skillet, cook the chicken with the onion over medium heat until browned.
2. In a bowl, whisk together soy sauce, mirin, sugar, sake, and teriyaki sauce.
3. Pour the sauce over the chicken and cook until it thickens and the chicken is fully cooked.
4. Pour the beaten eggs over the chicken and cover the pan to let the eggs set, about 2-3 minutes.
5. Serve the chicken and eggs over steamed rice and garnish with green onions.

Chashu Pork for Ramen

Ingredients:

- 1 lb pork belly, rolled and tied
- 3 cups water
- 2 tbsp soy sauce
- 2 tbsp sake
- 1 tbsp mirin
- 1 tbsp sugar
- 1-inch piece of ginger, sliced
- 2 garlic cloves, smashed

Instructions:

1. In a pot, combine all ingredients and bring to a simmer.
2. Add the pork belly and simmer for 1.5-2 hours, until the pork is tender and flavorful.
3. Let the pork cool in the broth, then slice thinly to serve with ramen.
4. Optionally, drizzle some of the braising liquid over the pork for added flavor.

Kushi Katsu (Skewered Fried Meats)

Ingredients:

- 1 lb pork or chicken, cut into bite-sized pieces
- 1 cup panko breadcrumbs
- 1 egg, beaten
- 1/2 cup flour
- 1/4 cup cornstarch
- Salt and pepper to taste
- Skewers
- Oil for frying
- Tonkatsu sauce for dipping

Instructions:

1. Thread the pork or chicken onto skewers.
2. In a bowl, mix flour, cornstarch, salt, and pepper. Dredge the skewered meat in the flour mixture, then dip in the beaten egg, and coat in panko breadcrumbs.
3. Heat oil in a deep pan or fryer to 350°F (175°C). Fry the skewers until golden brown and crispy, about 3-4 minutes.
4. Serve with tonkatsu sauce for dipping.

Matcha Latte and Mochi Desserts

For Matcha Latte:

- 1 tsp matcha powder
- 1 cup milk (or non-dairy milk)
- 1 tbsp honey or sugar
- 1/4 tsp vanilla extract (optional)

Instructions:

1. In a small bowl, whisk the matcha powder with a little hot water to form a smooth paste.
2. Heat the milk in a saucepan until hot but not boiling.
3. Add the matcha paste and honey to the milk and stir until fully combined.
4. Pour into a cup and enjoy with a sprinkle of matcha powder on top.

For Mochi:

- 1 cup mochiko (sweet rice flour)
- 1/2 cup sugar
- 1 cup water
- Cornstarch for dusting

Instructions:

1. In a bowl, mix mochiko, sugar, and water until smooth.

2. Pour the mixture into a heatproof bowl and steam for 30-40 minutes until the dough becomes sticky and thick.

3. Let the dough cool, then divide into small pieces and dust with cornstarch to prevent sticking.

4. Shape into balls or flatten them and fill with red bean paste (anko) if desired.